Bessie,

A Bassett Hound with Heart

Written by: Diane Baxter Trapeni

Illustrated by: Angela Reed Hinchey

ISBN: 9798664472172

Keep an eye out for these other exciting titles:

Nellie the Nibbler

Alice the Guinea Pig

Penny the Python

Jeremiah, a Song Bird

Vincent

Hubert

Phil Harmonic

Jeff Sticks up for his Buddies

Cord, Glue and 8 Screws

A Three Piggie Circus

DEDICATION

To my lovely cousin, Michele, who cares

deeply for every living being.

Whenever she is needed, she is there.

With love, cousin Diane. DMBT

I want to dedicate the illustrations to Emma, who lives with two expert rug braiders and a cat named Moe on a hill in Wallingford, VT. She loves to be part of the conversation, and will let out a loud bark when she thinks she is being ignored! ARH

Bessie's birthday is today. She's 12 just like your sister only in dog years it's around a gazillion.   She's been a devoted companion all her life.

She's gentle and so very affectionate, sweet-tempered and friendly. She's such a nice pal to have by your feet.

She is getting on in years now...Old Bessie.
She's lost a few teeth.

She **walks really slowly**, dragging her
belly on the porch to get to her favorite
spot...**and she tears up a lot lately.**

I think she misses Grandpa. Grandpa
is in the nursing home now.
He's old too. He's been with Bessie all
her dog life and now she mopes
around looking for him.

He mopes around
looking for her too.
Where's his favorite chair?
Where are his slippers?

Where are Bessie's toys?
Where is Bessie?
Where's the front porch?

Grandpa doesn't understand why his home doesn't look familiar.

It smells funny here and it's full of "old" people.

Did he get transported by aliens to this alien planet?

Why is he here?

Are they studying him, he wondered?

Bessie and Grandpa have a connection...like a psychic connection, you might say... They can kind of "read" each-other's minds.

Bessie wanted to see grandpa so she lumbered down the porch steps and went down the road about as fast as a turtle.

(That's where the car went two days ago with Grandpa inside and he is NOT in the house!)

She walked step-by-step, closer to the man she loved. It took her three years, or maybe, thirty minutes, to get to town. She was so close, she could smell him. (She was still a wonderful tracker!)

She could feel him now. She was getting closer. Just 6 more steps and she'd be with him. She could hardly make it to the top!

This porch was newer than her porch.
It had lots of rocking chairs on it.

There was only one man sitting on the porch. GRAMPS!!! The love of her life…

She'd never leave his
side again!
Ever!

The End

(of wondering and worrying…just do something!)

Keep an eye out for these other exciting Children's Books:

Penny the Enormous Python

Floyd the Colorful Chameleon

Francesca the Tropical Red-eyed Green Frog

Joe's Got Spots

Merrill the Squirrel and Jen the Hen:

Part 6 Brittany's Back!!!

Josephine, the Racehorse

Alice the Guinea Pig

Frances, a Gifted Frog for Sure!

Saffire. (Butterfly)

Serendipity. (Fish)

Jeremiah, the Song Bird

Christmas at the Castle

We are proud to introduce: ROSE

Rose

Rose was strong, determined and deliberate...

She knew what she wanted and she did whatever was

necessary to live her dream.

She has NO REGRETS!

About the TrapStone LLC: Owner and Author…

My name is Miss Diane. I taught for 42 years and have read thousands of books aloud to children.

I enjoyed that so much, I decided to write and illustrate books for you myself.

Enjoy!!!

About the Illustrator…

Angela Reed Hinchey was an art teacher for thirty years. She is a native Vermonter who lives in her four-generation family home. She never passes up an opportunity to visit an art museum and always has her sketch pad handy. She finds her old Queen Anne sun porch a wonderful place to sketch!

About the TrapStone LLC: Manager…

Ken Stone Sr. is a computer programmer and a business partner extraordinaire. He put my words, pictures and computer magic together so you could meet, Bessie, A Bassett Hound with Heart.